The

SECRET

D0913806

"*There does not exist and never will exist a creature in whom God, either within or without Himself, is so highly exalted as He is in the most Blessed Virgin Mary, not excepting the Saints or the Cherubim or the highest Seraphim in Paradise. Mary is the paradise of God and His unspeakable world.*"

—St. Louis De Montfort

The
SECRET
OF MARY

By
St. Louis De Montfort

"Happy, a thousand times happy, is the soul here below to which the Holy Ghost reveals the Secret of Mary . . ."

—St. Louis De Montfort

TAN BOOKS AND PUBLISHERS, INC.
Rockford, Illinois 61105

Imprimi potest: A. Josselin, S.M.M.
                  Superior General

Nihil obstat: Thomas W. Smiddy, S.T.L.

Imprimatur: ✠ Thomas Edmund Molloy, S.T.D.
                  Bishop of Brooklyn
                  Brooklyn, New York
                  June 14, 1947

Published by Montfort Publications, Bay Shore, New York, in 1940. Revised edition published by Montfort Publications in 1947. Retypeset and republished in 1998 by TAN Books and Publishers, Inc.

Over 1 million copies sold in the edition available from Montfort Publications.

ISBN 0-89555-617-0

Library of Congress Catalog Card No.: 98-60283

Cover illustration: Mother of Good Counsel (rendition by P. Sarullo).

Printed and bound in the United States of America.

TAN BOOKS AND PUBLISHERS, INC.
P.O. Box 424
Rockford, Illinois 61105
1998

"GOD ALONE."

—St. Louis De Montfort

CONTENTS

—Part I—
THE SECRET OF MARY

Introduction: A Secret of Sanctity 3
  I. Our Sanctification: Necessity of Sanctifying
        Ourselves 7
 II. Our Sanctification through Mary: A Necessary
        Means 10
III. Our Sanctification by the Perfect Devotion
        to the Blessed Virgin Mary,
        or The Holy Slavery of Love 22
        A. Nature and Scope 24
        B. Excellence 29
        C. Interior Practice 35
        D. Exterior Practices 46
 IV. The Tree of Life: Its Culture and Growth . . . 48

—Part II—
CONSECRATION TO JESUS THROUGH MARY

  I. First Period
        Twelve Preliminary Days—Renouncement
        of the World 56
 II. Second Period
        First Week—Knowledge of Self 57

Second Week—Knowledge of
    the Blessed Virgin 59
Third Week—Knowledge of Jesus Christ . . 60
Prayers 61
Act of Consecration 83

—Part III—
THE CONFRATERNITY OF MARY, QUEEN OF ALL HEARTS

The Confraternity of Mary, Queen of
    All Hearts 89

ABOUT ST. LOUIS
DE MONTFORT

St. Louis Marie Grignion de la Bacheleraie, who abandoned his family name for that of his birthplace, was born on January 31, 1673 in the little town of Montfort-la-Canne, which is located in Brittany, France. He studied for the priesthood at St. Sulpice in Paris, having made the 200-mile journey there on foot. He was ordained a priest in 1700, at the age of 27.

St. Louis De Montfort had wanted to become a missionary in Canada, but he was advised to remain in France. There he traveled around the western part of the country, from diocese to diocese and from parish to parish, instructing the people, preaching, helping the poor, hearing confessions, giving retreats, opening schools and rebuilding church buildings. His labors were almost miraculously fruitful. He stated that never did a sinner resist after being touched by him with a Rosary.

But because he encountered great opposition from religious authorities—in particular, being forbidden by the Bishop of Poitiers to preach in his diocese—he decided to travel to Rome to ask the Holy Father if he was doing God's Will and whether he should continue as before. St. Louis De Montfort walked to Rome—a thousand miles—and put his case to Pope Clement XI. The Pope told him to continue his traveling missionary work and named him Missionary Apostolic, but told him always to be sure to work under obedience to the diocesan authorities.

One of St. Louis De Montfort's greatest problems was the opposition he encountered from propagators of the Jansenist heresy, which was then very active in France. The Jansenists spread an atmosphere of harshness and moral rigorism, claiming that human nature was radically corrupted by Original Sin (as opposed to the Catholic teaching that human nature is still essentially good, though fallen, and although it has suffered a darkening of the intellect and weakening of the will). The Jansenists denied that God's mercy is available to all, and they allowed only infrequent reception of the Sacraments of Penance and the Holy Eucharist, and only after long and severe preparation—with Holy Communion being looked upon as a reward rather than a remedy. Also, they taught that God should always be addressed with fear and trembling. These tenets resembled those of Calvinism.

Although Jansenism had been condemned by the Church twice even before St. Louis De Montfort's birth, its teachings continued to spread and to influence people for a century. In contrast, St. Louis De Montfort preached confidence in Mary and union with her Divine Son.

St. Louis De Montfort founded two religious orders: the Daughters of Wisdom, begun in 1703 from a number of poor and afflicted girls at the Hospital of Poitiers, where he was temporary chaplain, and the Missionaries of the Company of Mary (Montfort Fathers and Brothers), founded in 1715. The Brothers of St. Gabriel, a teaching order, also claim St. Louis De Montfort as their spiritual father.

St. Louis De Montfort left several writings, the most famous being *The Secret of the Rosary, True Devotion to Mary,* and *The Secret of Mary.* These books were based on sermons he had given when traveling around France. By spreading devotion to the Blessed Virgin Mary, St. Louis De Montfort was teaching souls to love the devil's great enemy. (In *True Devotion to Mary*, he states that the devil fears Mary more than all angels and men, and in a sense more than God Himself.) At the Saint's beatification investigation, many witnesses testi-fied that during his life they had heard struggles between him and the devil, including the sound of fist blows and the swish of whips.

St. Louis De Montfort exhausted his great physical strength by his apostolic labors. On his deathbed in Saint-Laurent-sur-Sèvre, at age 43, he kissed the crucifix and a statue of the Blessed Mother. Apparently speaking to the devil, he exclaimed: "In vain do you attack me; I am between Jesus and Mary! I have finished my course: All is over. I shall sin no more!" Then he died peacefully on April 28, 1716. His feast day is April 28, the day of his birth in Heaven. St. Louis De Montfort's writings were examined by the Holy See, which pronounced that there was nothing in them to hinder his beatification and canonization. He was canonized in 1947.

The
SECRET
OF MARY

"Mary is the admirable echo of God.
When we say, 'Mary,' she answers, 'God.'
When, with St. Elizabeth, we call her
'Blessed,' she glorifies God."
                    —St. Louis De Montfort

—Part I—

THE SECRET OF MARY

DOCTRINE OF THE HOLY SLAVERY

INTRODUCTION

A SECRET OF SANCTITY

Conditions

1. Predestinate soul, here is a secret the Most High has taught me, which I have not been able to find in any book, old or new.[1] I confide it to you, by the inspiration of the Holy Ghost, on condition:

1° That you communicate it only to those who deserve it by their prayers, their alms-deeds and mortifications, by the persecutions they suffer, by their detachment from the world and their zeal for

---

1. The holy slavery of Jesus in Mary was known, no doubt, before St. Louis De Montfort's time; yet he rightly calls this devotion *a secret*: first, because there lies in it, as in all things supernatural, a hidden treasure which grace alone can help us to find and utilize; secondly, because there are but few souls that enter into the spirit of this devotion and go beyond its exterior practices. Again, as no one had as yet thoroughly explained this devotion nor shaped it into a definite method of spiritual life, St. Louis De Montfort could say of a truth, "I have not been able to find this secret in any book, old or new."

the salvation of souls.[2]

2° That you make use of it for your personal sanctification and salvation, for this secret works its effect in a soul only in proportion to the use made of it. Beware, then, of remaining inactive while possessing my secret; it would turn into a poison and be your condemnation.[3]

3° That you thank God all the days of your life

---

2. These words show how highly St. Louis De Montfort esteemed this devotion. As there are professional secrets committed only to men who know how to appreciate and exploit them, so this secret of sanctity must be entrusted only to such souls as truly concern themselves with their perfection; and following the recommendation of Our Lord not to profane holy things (*Matt.* 7:6), De Montfort preserves this secret with a holy jealousy that denotes respect for divine things.

3. "This solemn warning of the Saint is an application of the Parable of the Talents reported in *Matthew* 25. The unfaithful servant buried the talent he received and was condemned by the Master for his culpable negligence and for his disdain for the gifts of God. It is also a condemnation of the passivity or inertia taught by the false spirituality of Quietism or Semiquietism that existed in St. De Montfort's time and that was condemned by Rome. The Saint does not mean that one is obliged to follow his plan of spiritual life in order to be saved, for in his *Treatise on the True Devotion to Mary*, which is a development of the *Secret of Mary*, he explicitly says that we can attain divine union by other roads, but that his method is an EASY, SHORT, PERFECT and SECURE WAY that leads us to union with Our Lord."

for the grace He has given you to know a secret you do not deserve to know.

As you go on making use of this secret in the ordinary actions of your life, you will comprehend its value and its excellence, which at first you will not fully understand because of your many and grievous sins and because of your secret attachment to self.[4]

2. Before you read any further, lest you should be carried away by a too eager and natural desire to know this truth, kneel down and say devoutly the *Ave Maris Stella*[5] and the *Veni Creator*,[6] in order to understand and appreciate this divine mystery.[7]

---

4. These words contain three important counsels: 1) This devotion must be practiced in the ordinary course of life as well as in the most important actions. 2) Only when we steadily persevere in it, and not merely try it for a few weeks, shall we be able to judge of its excellence and know its fruit. 3) It is necessary to remove all hindrances to this devotion, namely, sin and secret affection for that which is sinful.

5. Page 63.

6. Page 61.

7. Let us not make light of this recommendation. It is an important one. If many persons do not become acquainted with the secret of this devotion, it is because they forget that in order to be allowed to enter this "Garden Enclosed," as Mary is called, they must entreat the Holy Ghost, "who searcheth all things, yea, the deep things of God" (*1 Cor.* 2: 10), to grant them that favor. (See *The Tree of Life*, p. 48; also *Prayer to Jesus,* p. 80.)

As I have not much time for writing, nor you for reading, I shall say everything as briefly as possible.

Note: The numerals in bold type were added by the Montfort Fathers to facilitate reference to this book; numerals which St. Louis De Montfort included in the text are indicated by a degree sign (for example, 1°).—*Publisher*, 1998.

I

OUR SANCTIFICATION

NECESSITY OF SANCTIFYING OURSELVES

The Will of God

3. Faithful soul, living image of God, redeemed by the Precious Blood of Jesus Christ, it is the will of God that you be holy like Him in this life and glorious like Him in the next. Your sure vocation is the acquisition of the holiness of God, and unless all your thoughts and words and actions, all the sufferings and events of your life tend to that end, you are resisting God by not doing that for which He has created you and is now preserving you.[1] Oh, what an admirable work! To change that which is dust into light, to make pure that which

---

1. Those who begin this devotion are here reminded of the recommendation of the masters of the spiritual life, namely, that the interior life must be their chief concern. They must be determined to obtain good results bought with the price of sacrifice. Compare these words with St . Louis De Montfort's advice on cultivating *The Tree of Life,* page 48.

is unclean, holy that which is sinful, to make the creature like its Creator, man like God! Admirable work, I repeat, but difficult in itself, and impossible to mere nature; only God by His grace, by His abundant and extraordinary grace, can accomplish it. Even the creation of the whole world is not so great a masterpiece as this.

Means of Sanctification

4. Predestinate soul, how are you to do it? What means will you choose to reach the height to which God calls you? The means of salvation and sanctification are known to all; they are laid down in the Gospel, explained by the masters of the spiritual life, practiced by the Saints, and necessary to all who wish to be saved and to attain perfection. They are humility of heart, continual prayer, mortification in all things, abandonment to Divine Providence and conformity to the will of God.

5. To practice all these means of salvation and sanctification, the grace of God is absolutely necessary. No one can doubt that God gives His grace to all, in a more or less abundant measure. I say in a more or less abundant measure, for God, although infinitely good, does not give equal grace to all, yet to each soul He gives sufficient grace.

The faithful soul will, with great grace, perform a great action, and with less grace a lesser action. It is the value and the excellence of the grace bestowed by God and corresponded to by the soul that gives to our actions their value and their excellence. These principles are certain.

An Easy Means

6. It all comes to this, then: that you should find an easy means for obtaining from God the grace necessary to make you holy; and this means I wish to make known to you. Now, I say that to find this grace of God, *we must find Mary.*[2]

---

2. This is characteristic of St. Louis De Montfort's devotion and makes it a special method of spiritual life.

II

OUR SANCTIFICATION
THROUGH MARY[1]

A NECESSARY MEANS

Mary Alone Has Found Grace with God

7. 1° Mary alone has found grace with God, both for herself and for every man in particular. The patriarchs and prophets and all the Saints of the Old Law were not able to find that grace.

Mother of Grace

8. 2° Mary gave being and life to the Author of all grace, and that is why she is called the Mother of Grace.

---

1. The reasons given here to prove that Mary is the most perfect means for finding Jesus are a condensed treatise on Mariology. If the faithful meditate on these points, they will come to understand the function assigned to Our Lady, by virtue of her divine maternity, in the mystery of the Incarnation and now in the whole Church.

Mary Has Received the Plenitude of Grace

9. 3° God the Father, from Whom every perfect gift and all grace come, as from its essential source, has given all graces to Mary by giving her His Son, so that, as St. Bernard says, "With His Son and in Him, God has given His Will to Mary."

Universal Treasurer of God's Graces

10. 4° God has entrusted Mary with the keeping, the administration and distribution of all His graces, so that all His graces and gifts pass through her hands; and (according to the power she has received over them), as St. Bernardine teaches, Mary gives to whom she wills, the way she wills, when she wills and as much as she wills, the graces of the Eternal Father, the virtues of Jesus Christ and the gifts of the Holy Ghost.

Mother of God's Children

11. 5° As in the order of nature a child must have a father and a mother, so likewise in the order of grace, a true child of the Church must have God for his Father and Mary for his Mother; and if any one should glory in having God for his Father and yet has not the love of a true child for

Mary, he is a deceiver, and the only father he has is the devil.

Mary Forms the Members of Jesus

12. 6° Since Mary has formed Jesus Christ, the Head of the elect, it is also her office to form the members of that Head, that is to say, all true Christians; for a mother does not form the head without the members, nor the members without the head. Whoever, therefore, wishes to be a member of Jesus Christ, full of grace and truth, must be formed in Mary by means of the grace of Jesus Christ, which she possesses in its fullness, in order to communicate it fully to her children, the true members of Jesus Christ.[2]

Through Her the Holy Ghost Produces the Elect

13. 7° As the Holy Ghost has espoused Mary and has produced in her, by her and from her, His

---

2. Conclude from this that we call Mary our Mother not because of mere feelings of piety and gratitude awakened in us by the conviction that she loves and protects us, but because she *is* our Mother in the spiritual order as truly as she is the Mother of Christ in the natural order. The spiritual motherhood of Mary, a consequence of her divine motherhood, is one of the truths on which the True Devotion of St. Louis De Montfort is founded.

masterpiece, Jesus Christ, the Word Incarnate, and has never repudiated His spouse, so He now continues to produce the elect, in her and by her, in a mysterious but real manner.

Mary Nourishes Souls and Gives Them Growth in God

14. 8° Mary has received a special office and power over our souls in order to nourish them and give them growth in God. St. Augustine even says that, during their present life, all the elect are hidden in Mary's womb and that they are not truly born until the Blessed Mother brings them forth to life eternal. Consequently, just as the child draws all its nourishment from the mother, who gives it in proportion to the child's weakness, in like manner do the elect draw all their spiritual nourishment and strength from Mary.

Mary Dwells in the Elect

15. 9° It is to Mary that God the Father said: "My daughter, let thy dwelling be in Jacob," that is, in My elect, prefigured by Jacob. It is to Mary that God the Son said: "My dear Mother, in Israel is thine inheritance," that is, in the elect. And it is to Mary that the Holy Ghost said: "Take root, My faithful spouse, in My elect." Whoever, then, is elect and predestinate has the Blessed Virgin with him, dwelling in his soul,[3] and he will allow her to plant there the roots of profound humility, of ardent charity and of every virtue.

Mary Forms Jesus in Us
A Living Mold of God

16. 10° St. Augustine calls Mary the living "mold of God," and that indeed she is; for it was in her alone that God was made a true man without losing any feature of the Godhead, and it is also in her alone that man can be truly formed

---

3. This abode of Mary in our soul may be explained in the following manner: Her presence in us cannot be compared to that of God living in our soul by Sanctifying Grace and thus making us partakers of His divine life. Neither must we believe that Mary is bodily present in our soul. Some have wrongfully charged St. Louis De Montfort with inferring the omnipresence of Mary. But let us bear in mind Mary's privilege of being truly the Mother of God (which privilege is hers personally and exclusively). As a consequence of that privilege, Mary beholds our souls in a universal manner and more excellently than the Saints and Angels do in their heavenly glory, and she is with us really, individually, intimately. Thus, we are morally present to her, and she is morally present to us, because by her prayers, her attention and her influence she cooperates with the Holy Ghost in forming Jesus in our souls. By way of comparison, we might say that Mary is present in our souls as the sun is present in a room by its light and warmth, even though it is not there itself.

into God, in so far as that is possible for human nature, by the grace of Jesus Christ.

A sculptor has two ways of making a lifelike statue or figure: he may carve the figure out of some hard, shapeless material, using for this purpose his professional skill and knowledge, his strength and the necessary instruments, or he may cast it in a mold. The first manner is long and difficult and subject to many mishaps; a single blow of the hammer or the chisel, awkwardly given, may spoil the whole work. The second is short, easy and smooth; it requires but little work and slight expense, provided the mold be perfect and made to reproduce the figure exactly; provided, moreover, the material used offer no resistance to the hand of the artist.[4]

A Perfect Mold

17. Mary is the great mold of God, made by the Holy Ghost to form a true God-Man by the Hypostatic Union and to form also a man-God

---

4. Therefore great docility is required on our part if we would be "formed quickly, easily and gently." This comparison of the mold explains very well the interior practice of this devotion. The devotion consists essentially in one single act which, under various forms and conditions, we apply to our whole life, both interior and exterior. Such is the simplicity of St. Louis De Montfort's method.

by grace. In that mold none of the features of the Godhead is wanting. Whoever is cast in it, and allows himself to be molded, receives all the features of Jesus Christ, true God. The work is done gently, in a manner proportioned to human weakness, without much pain or labor, in a sure manner, free from all illusion, for where Mary is the devil has never had and never will have access; finally, it is done in a holy and spotless manner, without a shadow of the least stain of sin.

Well-Molten Souls

18. Oh what a difference between a soul which has been formed in Christ by the ordinary ways of those who, like the sculptor, trust in their own skill and ingenuity, and a soul thoroughly tractable, entirely detached and well-molten, which, without trusting to its own skill, casts itself into Mary, there to be molded by the Holy Ghost. How many stains and defects and illusions, how much darkness and how much human nature is there in the former; and oh how pure, how heavenly and how Christlike is the latter!

Paradise and World of God

19. There does not exist and never will exist a

creature in whom God, either within or without Himself, is so highly exalted as He is in the most Blessed Virgin Mary, not excepting the Saints or the Cherubim or the highest Seraphim in Paradise. Mary is the paradise of God and His unspeakable world, into which the Son of God has come to work His wonders, to watch over it and to take His delight in it. God has made a world for wayfaring man, which is that world in which we dwell; He has made one for man in his glorified state, which is Heaven; and He has made one for Himself, which He has called Mary. It is a world unknown to most mortals here below and incomprehensible even to the Angels and Blessed in Heaven above, who, seeing God so highly exalted above them all and so deeply hidden in Mary, His world, are filled with admiration and unceasingly exclaim: "Holy, Holy, Holy."

God Alone in Her

20. Happy, a thousand times happy, is the soul here below to which the Holy Ghost reveals the Secret of Mary in order that it may come to know her; to which He opens the "Garden Enclosed" [*Cant.* 4:12], that it may enter into it; to which He gives access to that "Fountain Sealed," that it may draw from it and drink deep draughts of the living waters of grace! That soul will find God alone in His most amiable creature. It will find God infinitely holy and exalted, yet at the same time adapting Himself to its own weakness. Since God is present everywhere, He may be found everywhere, even in Hell, but nowhere do we creatures find Him nearer to us and more adapted to our weakness than in Mary, since it was for that end that He came and dwelt in her. Everywhere else He is the Bread of the strong, the Bread of the Angels, but in Mary He is the Bread of children.[5]

No Hindrance to Our Union with God

21. Let us not imagine, then, as some do who are misled by erroneous teachings, that Mary, being a creature, is a hindrance to our union with the Creator. It is no longer Mary who lives, it is Jesus Christ, it is God alone who lives in her. Her

---

5. This beautiful expression interprets the invitation of Divine Wisdom: "Come, eat the bread and drink the wine which I have mingled for you." (*Prov.* 9:5). It also accounts for the unexpected graces which this devotion draws upon those who persevere in its practice. Note that this method of spiritual formation is practically the same as the education given by a mother to her child. In ourselves we experience the infirmities and the wants of infancy, in Mary we find the strong and never wearied love of a mother. All that we have to do is to abandon ourselves to Mary and to remain dependent on her in all things, just like children.

transformation into God surpasses that of St. Paul [*Gal.* 2:20] and of the other Saints more than the heavens surpass the earth by their height. Mary is made for God alone, and far from ever detaining a soul in herself, she casts the soul upon God and unites it with Him so much the more perfectly as the soul is more perfectly united to her. Mary is the admirable echo of God. When we say, "Mary," she answers, "God." When, with St. Elizabeth, we call her "Blessed," she glorifies God. If the falsely enlightened, whom the devil has so miserably illusioned, even in prayer, had known how to find Mary, and through her to find Jesus, and through Jesus, God the Father, they would not have had such terrible falls. The Saints tell us that when we have once found Mary, and through Mary, Jesus, and through Jesus, God the Father, we have found all good. He who says *all,* excepts nothing: all grace and all friendship with God, all safety from God's enemies, all truth to crush falsehoods, all facility to overcome difficulties in the way of salvation, all comfort and all joy amidst the bitterness of life.

She Imparts the Grace to Carry Crosses

22. This does not mean that he who has found Mary by a true devotion will be exempt from crosses and sufferings.[6] Far from it; he is more besieged by them than others are, because Mary, the Mother of the living, gives to all her children portions of the Tree of Life, which is the Cross of Jesus. But along with their crosses she also imparts the grace to carry them patiently and even cheerfully; and thus it is that the crosses which she lays upon those who belong to her are rather steeped in sweetness than filled with bitterness. If for a while her children feel the bitterness of the cup which one must needs drink in order to be the friend of God, the consolation and joy which this good Mother sends after the trial encourage them exceedingly to carry still heavier and more painful crosses.

Conclusion

23. The difficulty, then, is to find really and truly the most Blessed Virgin Mary in order to find all abundant grace. God, being the absolute Master, can confer directly by Himself that which

---

6. St. Louis De Montfort has explained that his true devotion is an easy means of sanctification, yet he wishes to guard us against the common illusion that his method exempts us from spiritual labor and sufferings. He is himself a striking example of the manly education which Mary, the valiant woman, gives to her children, as well as of the love of Jesus crucified which she enkindles in their hearts.

He usually grants only through Mary. It would even be rash to deny that sometimes He does so. Nevertheless, St. Thomas teaches that in the order of grace, established by Divine Wisdom, God ordinarily communicates Himself to men only through Mary. Therefore, if we would go up to Him and be united with Him, we must use the same means He used to come down to us, to be made man and to impart His graces to us. That means is a true devotion [perfect devotion] to our Blessed Lady.

III

OUR SANCTIFICATION BY THE PERFECT DEVOTION TO THE BLESSED VIRGIN MARY

OR

THE HOLY SLAVERY OF LOVE

A PERFECT MEANS

Devotions to Mary

24. There are several true devotions to Our Lady: here I do not speak of those that are false.

1. Devotion without Special Practices

25. The first consists in fulfilling our Christian duties, avoiding mortal sin, acting more out of love than fear, praying to Our Lady now and then, honoring her as the Mother of God, yet without having any special devotion to her.

2. Devotion with Special Practices

26. The second consists in entertaining for Our Lady more perfect feelings of esteem and love, of confidence and veneration. It leads us to join the Confraternities of the Holy Rosary and of the Scapular, to recite the five decades or the fifteen decades of the Rosary, to honor Mary's images and altars, to publish her praises and to enroll ourselves in her sodalities.[1] This devotion is good, holy and praiseworthy, if we keep ourselves free from sin; but it is not so perfect as the next, nor so efficient in severing our soul from creatures or in detaching us from ourselves, in order to be united with Jesus Christ.

3. The Perfect Devotion: The Holy Slavery of Love

27. The third devotion to Our Lady, known and practiced by very few persons, is the one I am now about to disclose to you, predestinate soul.

---

1. All such devotions, remarks St. Louis De Montfort elsewhere, include but a limited number of devout practices and take up but a part of our daily life, while the one he proposes embraces our whole life and divests us of all things.

A. NATURE AND SCOPE OF THE HOLY SLAVERY OF LOVE

Nature

28. It consists in giving oneself entirely and as a slave to Mary, and to Jesus through Mary; and after that to do all that we do, with Mary, in Mary, through Mary and for Mary.[2] I shall now explain these words.

Scope: Total Surrender

29. We should choose a special feast-day on which we give, consecrate and sacrifice to Mary voluntarily, lovingly and without constraint, entirely and without reserve: our body and soul, our exterior property, such as house, family and income; and also our interior and spiritual

---

2. We must, therefore, note two things in this devotion: first, an *act* of total consecration to Jesus through Mary; and secondly, a *state* of being consecrated. That state consists in the permanent disposition of living and acting habitually in dependence on Mary; and that is called the spirit or the interior part of this consecration. This practice, although it embraces our entire life, appears so small and trifling at first glance, that St. Louis De Montfort has justly compared it to the mustard seed. But one comes to realize its vital energy and its wonderful effects when it has grown strong by persistent exercise.

possessions; namely, our merits, graces, virtues and satisfactions.[3]

It should be observed here that by this devotion the soul sacrifices to Jesus, through Mary, all that it holds most dear, things of which even no religious order would require the sacrifice; namely, the right to dispose of ourselves, of the value of our prayers and alms, of our mortifications and satisfactions. The soul leaves everything to be freely disposed of by Our Lady so that she may apply it all according to her own will for the greater glory of God, which she alone knows perfectly.

Surrender of the Value of Our Good Works

30. We leave to her disposal all the satisfactory and impetratory value of our good works, so that after we have made the sacrifice of them— although not by vow—we are no longer the masters of any good works we may do; but Our Lady may apply them, sometimes for the relief or the deliverance of a soul in Purgatory, sometimes

---

3. These words show us the far-reaching effect of this consecration, which St. Louis De Montfort calls a perfect renewal of the baptismal vows; and, indeed, in making it we give ourselves anew to Jesus Christ, Our Lord, through the hands of Mary.

for the conversion of a poor sinner, etc.[4]

31. By this devotion we also place our merits in the hands of Our Lady, but only that she may preserve, augment and embellish them, because we cannot communicate to one another either the merits of sanctifying grace or those of glory. However, we give her all our prayers and good works, inasmuch as they have an impetratory and satisfactory value, that she may distribute and

---

4. It may not be amiss to give here a short explanation of the Heroic Act of Charity, and to point out in what it differs from this act of consecration.

According to a definition of the Sacred Congregation of Indulgences (December, 1885), the Heroic Act of Charity consists in this: that a member of the Church Militant offers to God, for the souls in Purgatory, all the satisfactory works which he will perform during his lifetime and also all the suffrages which may accrue to him after his death.

By the Act of Consecration to Jesus through Mary as taught by St. Louis De Montfort, we give to Our Lady not only the satisfactory works of our life, but all else, nothing excepted (see the Act of Consecration, p. 83). The use to be made of our good works and satisfactions is not determined by us, as it is in the Heroic Act, but it is left to Mary's intention and will. In his Act of Consecration, St. Louis De Montfort does not seem to comprise directly the suffrages which may accrue to us in Purgatory, but indirectly they are implied: "I leave to thee . . . all that belongs to me . . . in time and in eternity."

Neither the Heroic Act nor our Act of Consecration implies a vow, yet both may be made with a vow, if discretion and sound judgment are not lacking in making such a solemn promise to God.

apply them to whom she pleases. If, after having thus consecrated ourselves to Our Lady, we desire to relieve a soul in Purgatory, to save a sinner, or to assist a friend by our prayers, our alms-deeds, our mortifications and sacrifices, we must humbly ask it of Our Lady, abiding, however, by her decision, which remains unknown to us; and we must be fully persuaded that the value of our actions, being dispensed by the same hand which God Himself makes use of to distribute to us His graces and gifts, cannot fail to be applied for His greater glory.

Three Kinds of Slavery

32. I have said that this devotion consists in giving ourselves to Mary as slaves.[5] But notice that

---

5. These words show us the true nature of this consecration. By making it we place ourselves in a state in which we are owned by Jesus and Mary and are totally dependent on their will. Now that is the nature and the condition of a slave. But to remove the idea of there being any degradation or tyrannical violence in this noble servitude, St. Louis De Montfort explains that it is a voluntary slavery, full of honor and of love, giving us the liberty of the true children of God.

There is then no reason for being scared or repelled by the words "slave" and "slavery." Consider the *state,* not the *word* which expresses the state of total, of lasting and disinterested subjection and dependence on the Master through the Mother. One may ask why not use other words? It is because there are none to express adequately this special state of consecration.

there are three kinds of slavery. The first is the slavery of nature; in this sense all men, good and bad alike, are slaves of God. The second is the slavery of constraint; the devils and the damned are slaves of God in this second sense. The third is the slavery of love and of free will; and this is the one by which we must consecrate ourselves to God through Mary. It is the most perfect way for us human creatures to give ourselves to God our Creator.

Servant and Slave

33. Notice again, that there is a great difference between a servant and a slave. A servant claims wages for his services; a slave has a right to none. A servant is free to leave his master when he likes—he serves him only for a time; a slave belongs to his master for life and has no right to leave him. A servant does not give to his master the right of life and death over him; a slave gives himself up entirely, so that his master can put him to death without being molested by the law. It is easily seen, then, that he who is a slave by constraint is rigorously dependent on his master. Strictly speaking, a man must be dependent in that sense only on his Creator. Hence, we do not find that kind of slavery among Christians, but only among pagans.

Happiness of the Slave of Love

34. But happy and a thousand times happy is the generous soul that consecrates itself entirely to Jesus through Mary as a slave of love after it has shaken off by Baptism the tyrannical slavery of the devil!

B. EXCELLENCE OF THE HOLY SLAVERY OF LOVE

I should require much supernatural light to describe perfectly the excellence of this practice. I shall content myself with these few remarks.

Imitation of the Trinity

35. 1° To give ourselves to Jesus through Mary is to imitate God the Father, who has given us His Son only through Mary, and who communicates to us His grace only through Mary. It is to imitate God the Son, who has come to us only through Mary, and who, "by giving us an example, that as He has done, so we do also" (*John* 13:15), has urged us to go to Him by the same means by which He has come to us—that is, through Mary. It is to imitate the Holy Ghost, who bestows His graces and gifts upon us only through Mary. "Is it not fitting," asks St. Bernard, "that grace should return to its Author by the same channel which conveyed it to us?"

It Honors Jesus

36. 2° To go to Jesus through Mary is truly to honor Jesus Christ, for it denotes that we do not esteem ourselves worthy of approaching His infinite holiness directly and by ourselves because of our sins; that we need Mary, His holy Mother, to be our advocate and Mediatrix with Him, our Mediator. It is to approach Jesus as our Mediator and Brother, and at the same time to humble ourselves before Him, as before our God and our Judge. In a word, it is to practice humility, which is always exceedingly pleasing to the heart of God.

It Purifies and Embellishes Our Good Works

37. 3° To consecrate ourselves thus to Jesus through Mary is to place in Mary's hands our good actions, which although they may appear to us to be good, are often very imperfect and unworthy of the sight and the acceptance of God, before whom even the stars are not pure. Ah! Let us pray, then, to our dear Mother and Queen, that having received our poor present, she may purify it, sanctify it, embellish it and thus render it worthy of God. All that our soul possesses is of less value before God, the heavenly Householder, when it comes to winning His friendship and favor, than a worm-eaten apple presented to the king by a poor farmer in payment of the rent of his farm. But what would such a farmer do if he were wise and if he were well liked by the queen? Would he not give his apple to the queen? And would she not out of kindness to the poor man, as also out of respect for the king, remove from the apple all that is worm-eaten or spoiled, and then place it in a gold dish and surround it with flowers? Would the king refuse to accept the apple then? Or would he not rather receive it with joy from the hands of the queen, who favors that poor man? "If you wish to present something to God, no matter how small it may be," says St. Bernard, "place it in Mary's hands, if you do not wish to be refused."

38. Great God, how insignificant everything that we do really is! But let us place all in Mary's hands by this devotion. When we have given ourselves to Mary to the very utmost of our power, by despoiling ourselves completely in her honor, she will far outdo us in generosity and will repay us a hundredfold. She will communicate herself to us, with her merits and virtues; she will place our presents on the golden plate of her charity; she will clothe us, as Rebecca clothed Jacob, with the beautiful garments of her elder and only Son, Jesus Christ—that is, with His merits, which she has at her disposal; and thus, after we have despoiled ourselves of everything in her honor, we shall be "clothed in double garments"; that is, the garments, the ornaments, the perfumes, the merits and the virtues of Jesus and Mary clothe the soul of their slave, who has despoiled himself and who perseveres in his despoliation.[6]

Charity in the Highest Degree

39. 4° Moreover, to give ourselves thus to Our Lady is to practice charity towards our neighbor in the highest possible degree, because we give her all that we hold most dear and let her dispose of it at her will in favor of the living and the dead.

It Increases the Grace of God in Us

40. 5° By this devotion we place our graces, merits and virtues in safety, for we make Mary the

---

6. This charming comment on the words of St. Bernard will console and encourage certain souls who grow weary and sad when they become conscious of their unworthiness and their insufficiency. As St. Louis De Montfort loves to say, and his saying is very true, Mary will be "their supplement" with God.

depository of them all, saying to her: "See, my dear Mother, here are the good works that I have been able to do through the grace of thy dear Son; I am not able to keep them on account of my own weakness and inconstancy, and also because of the many wicked enemies who attack me day and night. Alas! One may see every day the cedars of Lebanon fall into the mire and the eagles, which had raised themselves to the sun, become birds of night; and so do a thousand of the just fall on my left hand and ten thousand on my right. But thou, my most powerful princess, sustain me lest I fall; keep all my possessions for fear I may be robbed of them. All I have I entrust to thee. I know well who thou art; therefore, I entrust myself entirely to thee; thou art faithful to God and to men; thou wilt not allow anything to perish that I entrust to thee; thou art powerful, and nothing can hurt thee nor rob thee of anything thou holdest in thy hands."[7] "When you follow Mary, you will not go astray; when you pray to her, you will not despair; when you think of her, you will not err; when she sustains you, you will not fall; when she

---

7. These words ought to be considered by all who are concerned about their perseverance in grace and their interior perfection. Many there are who hesitate even to begin and many who draw back soon after starting, because they apprehend a possible failure or lack of perseverance.

protects you, you will not fear; when she leads you, you will not become tired; when she favors you, you will arrive safely."[8] And again: "She keeps her Son from striking us; she keeps the devil from hurting us; she keeps our virtues from escaping us; she keeps our merits from being destroyed; she keeps our graces from being lost." These are the words of St. Bernard. They express in substance all I have said. Were there but this one motive to incite in me a desire for this devotion—namely, that it is a sure means of keeping me in the grace of God and even of increasing that grace in me, my heart ought to burn with longing for it.

It Renders the Soul Free

41. 6° This devotion truly frees the soul with the liberty of the children of God. Since for love of Mary we reduce ourselves freely to slavery, she, out of gratitude, will dilate our heart, intensify our love and cause us to walk with giant steps in the way of God's commandments. She delivers the soul from weariness, sadness and scruples. It was this devotion which Our Lord taught to Mother Agnes of Jesus[9] as a sure means of delivering her

---

8. St. Bernard, *Inter flores,* cap. 135, *de Maria Virgine.*
9. A Dominican nun who died in the odor of sanctity in the year 1634 at the convent of Langeac in Auvergne, France.

from the severe sufferings and perplexities which troubled her. "Make thyself," He said, "My Mother's slave." She did so, and in a moment her troubles ceased.

Obedience to the Counsels of the Church

42. To show that this devotion is rightfully authorized it would be necessary to mention the bulls of the Popes and the pastoral letters of the bishops, speaking in its favor; the indulgences granted to it; the confraternities established in its honor; the examples of the many Saints and illustrious persons who have practiced it. But all that I shall leave out.

C. INTERIOR PRACTICE OF THE HOLY SLAVERY OF LOVE

Its Guiding Formula

43. I have said that this devotion consists in doing all our actions with Mary, in Mary, through Mary and for Mary.

Scope of This Formula

44. It is not enough to have given ourselves once as slaves to Jesus through Mary, nor is it

enough to renew that act of consecration every month or every week. That alone would not make it a permanent devotion, nor could it bring the soul to that degree of perfection to which it is capable of raising it. It is not very difficult to enroll ourselves in a confraternity, nor to practice this devotion in as far as it prescribes a few vocal prayers every day; but the great difficulty is to enter into its spirit. Now its spirit consists in this, that we be interiorly dependent on Mary; that we be slaves of Mary, and through her, of Jesus.

I have found many people who, with admirable zeal, have adopted the exterior practices of this holy slavery of Jesus and Mary, but I have found only a few who have accepted its interior spirit, and still fewer who have persevered in it.

MEANING AND EXPLANATION OF THIS FORMULA

Act *with* Mary

45. 1° The essential practice of this devotion is to do all our actions *with* Mary. This means that we must take Our Lady as the perfect model of all that we do.

46. Before undertaking anything, we must renounce ourselves and our own views.[10] We must place ourselves as mere nothings before God, unable of ourselves to do anything that is supernaturally good or profitable to our salvation. We must have recourse to Our Lady, uniting ourselves to her and to her intentions, although they are not known to us; and through Mary we must unite ourselves to the intentions of Jesus Christ. In other words, we must place ourselves as instruments in the hands of Mary, that she may act in us and do with us and for us whatever she pleases, for the greater glory of her Son, and through the Son, for the glory of the Father; so that the whole work of our interior life and of our spiritual perfection is accomplished only by dependence on Mary.

---

10. From these indications, however abstract, we may learn that the act of union with Mary, as understood by St. Louis De Montfort, requires two things in the work of our sanctification: 1) the removal of all obstacles (sin and its occasions) by renouncing ourselves; 2) the union of our will with the will of God and of our actions with the impulse of divine grace. Without that self-renunciation in all things, our union with Mary would be very imperfect, our dependence on her would be an illusion (see 3, 4 and 5, *The Tree of Life*). Note also, that by telling us to renounce our own views and intentions, however good they be, in order to adopt those of Mary, De Montfort counsels the practice of that which is most perfect.

Act *in* Mary

47. 2° We must do all things *in* Mary;[11] that is to say, we must become accustomed little by little to recollect ourselves interiorly and thus try to form within us some idea or spiritual image of Mary.[12] She will be, as it were, the oratory of our soul, in which we offer up all our prayers to God, without fear of not being heard; she will be to us a Tower of David, in which we take refuge from all our enemies; a burning lamp to enlighten our interior and to inflame us with divine love; a sacred altar upon which we contemplate God in Mary and with her. In short, Mary will be the only means used by our soul in dealing with God;

---

11. *In* indicates an indwelling, an intimate union which produces unity. As St. Louis De Montfort expresses it, we must "enter into Mary's interior and stay there, adopting her views and feelings." Mary must become, as it were, the place and the atmosphere in which we live; her influence must penetrate us. As soon as this disposition of our soul has become habitual, we can say that we dwell in Mary, and having thus become as one moral person with her, we abide in her and she dwells in us, in the sense explained above (see note 3, p. 14).

12. St. Teresa gives similar advice to beginners for keeping recollected and united with Our Lord when at prayer. She recommends the use of images, and in this she is of the same mind as St. Louis De Montfort, who had recourse to images and banners, to the erection of calvaries and of other exterior displays that appeal to the senses and elevate the soul to God.

she will be our universal refuge. If we pray, we will pray in Mary; if we receive Jesus in Holy Communion, we will place Him in Mary, so that He may take His delight in her; if we do anything at all, we will act in Mary; everywhere and in all things we will renounce ourselves.

Act *through* Mary

48. 3° We must never go to Our Lord except *through* Mary, through her intercession and her influence with Him. We must never be without Mary when we pray to Jesus.

Act *for* Mary

49. 4° Lastly, we must do all our actions *for* Mary. This means that as slaves of this august princess, we must work only for her, for her interests and her glory— making this the immediate end of all our actions—and for the glory of God, which must be their final end. In everything we do, we must renounce our self-love, because very often self-love sets itself up in an imperceptible manner as the end of our actions. We should often repeat, from the bottom of our heart: "O my dear Mother! It is for thee that I go here or there; for thee that I do this or that; for thee that I suffer this pain or wrong."

PRACTICAL COUNSELS CONCERNING
THE SPIRIT OF THE HOLY SLAVERY

Not More Perfect to Go Straight to Jesus
without Mary

50. Beware, predestinate soul, of believing that it is more perfect to go straight to Jesus, straight to God. Without Mary, your action and your intention will be of little value; but if you go to God through Mary, your work will be Mary's work, and consequently it will be sublime and most worthy of God.[13]

Not Necessary to Feel and Enjoy
What You Say and Do

51. Moreover, do not try to feel and enjoy what you say and do, but say and do everything with that pure faith which Mary had on earth and

---

13. This does not mean that we may not approach Our Lord directly to speak to Him in prayer or contemplation; nor does it mean that in every action of ours we must think of Mary actually and distinctly; a virtual intention is sufficient. St. Louis De Montfort, indeed, says that our offering or act of consecration, if renewed but once a month or once a week (we might add, once a day), does not establish us in the spirit of this devotion, which is a state or a habit; yet he remarks that our interior look toward Mary, though it be but a general and hasty look, is sufficient to renew our offering.

which she will communicate to you in due time. Poor little slave, leave to your Sovereign Queen the clear sight of God, the raptures, the joys, the satisfactions and the riches of Heaven, and content yourself with pure faith, although full of repugnance, distractions, weariness and dryness, and say: "Amen, so be it," to whatever Mary, your Mother, does in Heaven. That is the best you can do for the time being.[14]

Not Necessary to Enjoy Immediately the Presence of Mary

52. Take great care also not to torment yourself should you not enjoy immediately the sweet presence of the Blessed Virgin in your soul, for this is a grace not given to all; and even when God, out of His great mercy, has thus favored a soul, it is always very easy to lose this grace, unless by frequent recollection the soul remains alive to that interior presence of Mary. Should this misfortune

---

14. Useful advice to those who are but beginning and who might think that they do nothing good because they do not see or feel. St. Louis De Montfort reminds them of the truth that our union with God consists in an act of the will. In his *True Devotion* he says that that act may be either mental or expressed in words; it can be made in the twinkling of an eye. In his prayer to Mary (found further on), he makes us ask for detachment of the senses in our devotion.

befall you, return calmly to your Sovereign Queen and make amends to her.[15]

WONDERFUL EFFECTS OF THIS INTERIOR PRACTICE

53. Experience will teach you much more about this devotion than I can tell you; and if you remain faithful to the little I have taught you, you will find so many rich fruits of grace in this practice that you will be surprised and filled with joy.

54. Let us set to work then, dear soul, and by the faithful practice of this devotion let us obtain the grace "that Mary's soul may be in us to glorify the Lord, that her spirit may be in us to rejoice in God," as St. Ambrose says. "Do not think that there was more glory and happiness in dwelling in Abraham's bosom, which was called Paradise, than

---

15. This interior presence of Mary is a favor St. Louis De Montfort enjoyed in an exceptional degree, as we may see by reading his life. He says: "It is a grace not given to all." Yet he exhorts us all to practice his true devotion and promises to all without exception "that Mary's soul will be in them." It is true, he always insists upon the condition of perseverance in practicing this devotion. As there are, however, but few souls who remain faithful to its spirit, even in a lower degree, we must say that this presence of Mary is not given to all.

in the bosom of Mary, in which God has placed His throne," as the learned Abbot Guerric says.

It Establishes Mary's Life in the Soul

55. This devotion, faithfully practiced, produces many happy effects in the soul. The most important of them all is that it establishes, even here below, Mary's life in the soul, so that it is no longer the soul that lives, but Mary living in it; for Mary's life becomes its life. And when, by an unspeakable yet real grace, the Blessed Virgin is Queen in a soul, what wonders does she not work there! She is the worker of great wonders, particularly in our soul, but she works them in secret, in a way unknown to the soul itself, for were it to know, it might destroy the beauty of her works.

Mary Causes Jesus to Live in That Soul

56. As Mary is the fruitful Virgin everywhere, she produces in the soul wherein she dwells purity of heart and body, purity of intention and of purpose, and fruitfulness in good works. Do not think, dear soul, that Mary, the most fruitful of all pure creatures, who has brought forth even a God, remains idle in a faithful soul. She will cause Jesus Christ to live in that soul, and the soul to live in constant union with Jesus Christ. "My dear children, with whom I am in labor again until Christ is formed in you." (*Gal.* 4:19). If Jesus Christ is the fruit of Mary in each individual soul, as well as in all souls in general, He is, however, her fruit and her masterpiece more particularly in a soul in which she dwells.

Mary Becomes Everything to That Soul

57. In fine, Mary becomes everything to that soul in the service of Jesus Christ. The mind will be enlightened by Mary's pure faith. The heart will be deepened by Mary's humility. It will be dilated and inflamed by Mary's charity; made clean by Mary's purity; noble and great by her motherly care. But why dwell any longer on this? Only experience can teach the wonders wrought by Mary, wonders so great that neither the wise nor the proud, nor even many of the devout can believe them.

SPECIAL FUNCTION OF THE HOLY SLAVERY IN THE LATTER TIMES

Through Mary, Jesus Will Reign

58. As it is through Mary that God came into the world the first time, in a state of humiliation and annihilation, may we not say that it is

through Mary also that He will come the second time, as the whole Church expects Him to come, to rule everywhere and to judge the living and the dead? Who knows how and when that will be accomplished? I do know that God, whose thoughts are as far removed from ours as Heaven is distant from the earth, will come in a time and a manner that men expect the least, even those who are most learned and most versed in Holy Scripture, which is very obscure on this subject.

59. We ought also to believe that toward the End of Time, and perhaps sooner than we think, God will raise up great men full of the Holy Ghost and imbued with the spirit of Mary, through whom this powerful Sovereign will work great wonders in the world, so as to destroy sin and to establish the Kingdom of Jesus Christ, her Son, upon the ruins of the kingdom of this corrupt world; and these holy men will succeed by means of this devotion, of which I do but give here the outline and which my deficiency only impairs.

D. EXTERIOR PRACTICES OF THE HOLY SLAVERY OF LOVE

60. Besides the interior practice of this devotion, of which we have just spoken, there are also certain exterior practices, which we must neither omit nor neglect.

Consecration and Renewal

61. The first one is to choose a special feastday on which to consecrate ourselves to Jesus through the Blessed Virgin Mary, whose slaves we make ourselves. On the same day we should receive Holy Communion for that intention, and spend the day in prayer. At least once a year, on the same day, we should renew our act of consecration.

A Token of Our Servitude

62. The second one is to pay to Our Lady, every year on that same day, some little tribute, as a token of our servitude and dependence; such has always been the homage paid by slaves to their masters. That tribute may consist of an act of mortification, an alms, a pilgrimage or some prayers. Bl. Marino, we are told by his brother, St. Peter Damian, was wont to take the discipline in public every year on the same day before the altar of Our Lady. Such zeal is not required, nor do we counsel it; but if we give but little to Mary, let us at least offer it with a humble and grateful heart.

Celebration of the Annunciation

63. The third practice is to celebrate every year, with special devotion, the feast of the Annunciation, which is the patronal feast of this devotion and was established to honor and imitate the dependence in which the Eternal Word placed Himself on that day out of love for us.

Recitation of the *Little Crown* and the *Magnificat*

64. The fourth external practice is to say every day (not, however, under pain of sin, in case of omission) the *Little Crown of the Blessed Virgin,* which is composed of three *Our Fathers* and twelve *Hail Marys*; also, often to recite the *Magnificat,* which is the only hymn of Mary that we possess, to thank God for His graces in the past and to beg of Him fresh blessings for the present. Above all, we ought not to fail to say this hymn in thanksgiving after Holy Communion. The learned Gerson tells us that Our Lady herself was wont to recite it after Communion.

IV
THE TREE OF LIFE:
ITS CULTURE AND ITS GROWTH
OR
HOW TO MAKE MARY LIVE AND REIGN IN OUR SOULS

Predestinate soul, have you understood, by the grace of the Holy Ghost, what I have tried to explain to you in the preceding pages? If so, be thankful to God, for it is a secret known and understood by only a few. If you have found the treasure hidden in the field of Mary, the precious pearl of the Gospel, sell all that you have in order to buy it. You must make the sacrifice of yourself to the Blessed Mother, you must disappear in her, so that you may find God alone.

If the Holy Ghost has planted in your soul the true Tree of Life, which is the devotion that I have just explained to you, you must do all you can to cultivate it, in order that it may yield its fruit in due season. This devotion is like the mustard seed of the Gospel, "which is the least indeed of all seeds, but when it is grown up, is greater than all herbs, and becometh a tree, so that the birds of the air (i.e., the predestinate) come and dwell in the branches thereof," and rest in its shade from the heat of the sun and hide there in safety from the beasts of prey.

This is the way, predestinate soul, to cultivate it:

No Human Support

1° This Tree, once planted in a faithful heart, requires the open air and freedom from all human support. Being heavenly, it must be kept clear from any creatures that might prevent it from lifting itself to God, in whom its origin lies. Hence, you must not rely on your own skill or your natural talents, on your own repute or the protection of men. You must have recourse to Mary and rely on her help alone.

Constant Concern of the Soul

2° The one in whose soul this Tree is planted must, like a good gardener, constantly watch over it and tend it, for it is a Tree that has life and is capable of yielding the fruit of life. Therefore, it must be cultivated and raised by the steady care and application of the soul; and the soul that would become perfect will make this its chief aim and occupation.

Violence to Oneself

3° Whatever is likely to choke the Tree or in the course of time prevent its yielding its fruit, such as thorns and thistles, must be cut away and rooted out. This means that by mortification and doing violence to ourselves, we must suppress and renounce all useless pleasures and vain traffic with creatures. In other words, we must crucify the flesh, keep recollected and mortify our senses.

No Self-Love

4° You must also keep watch on insects which might do harm to the Tree. These insects are self-love or love of comfort. They eat away the foliage of the Tree and destroy the fair hopes it gives of yielding fruit, for self-love is opposed to the love of Mary.

Horror of Sin

5° You must not allow destructive animals to approach the Tree of Life. By these animals are meant all sins. They may kill the Tree of Life by their touch alone. Even their breath must be kept away from it, namely, venial sins, for they are most dangerous if committed without regret.

Fidelity to Religious Practices

6° It is also necessary to water this heavenly Tree often with the fervor of piety in our religious practices, in our Confessions and Communions, in all our prayers, both public and private; otherwise, it will stop yielding fruit.

Peace in Trials

7° Do not become alarmed when the Tree is moved and shaken by the wind, for it is necessary that the storms of temptation should threaten to uproot it, that snow and ice should cover it, so as, if possible, to destroy it. This means that this devotion will of necessity be attacked and contradicted, but provided we persevere in cultivating it in our souls, we need not fear.

Its Fruit: Our Lord

Predestinate soul, if you thus cultivate the Tree of Life, freshly planted in your soul by the Holy Ghost, I assure you that in a short time it will grow so tall that the birds of Heaven will come to dwell in it. It will be a good tree, yielding fruit of honor and grace in due season, namely, the sweet and adorable Jesus, who always has been, and always will be, the only fruit of Mary.

Happy the soul in which Mary, the Tree of Life, is planted; happier the soul in which she has acquired growth and bloom; still happier the soul in which she yields her fruit; but most happy of all the soul which relishes and preserves Mary's fruit until death, and for ever and ever. Amen.

"He who holdeth (this), let him hold (it)."

GOD ALONE

—Part II—

CONSECRATION TO JESUS THROUGH MARY

CONSECRATION TO JESUS THROUGH MARY

St. Louis De Montfort advises us to prepare for the Consecration by exercises which certainly are not compulsory, but which assure its great efficacy, because of the purity and other dispositions which they tend to develop in our souls.

Two different periods are assigned for these exercises: a preliminary period of twelve days, during which we endeavor "to free ourselves from the spirit of the world"; then a second period of three weeks: the first devoted to the knowledge of ourselves; the second to knowledge of the Blessed Virgin; and the third to knowledge of Jesus Christ.

These periods mentioned by St. Louis De Montfort do not constitute a rigorous and unchangeable division. According to circumstances, they may be lengthened or shortened. The faithful often take but three days to prepare for the annual renewal of their Consecration.

The object of this Consecration is to cast off the spirit of the world, which is contrary to that of

Jesus Christ, in order to acquire fully the spirit of Jesus Christ through the Blessed Virgin. Hence the practices suggested by St. Louis De Montfort: renouncement of the world, knowledge of self, of the Blessed Virgin and of Jesus Christ.

—FIRST PERIOD—

Twelve Preliminary Days
RENOUNCEMENT OF THE WORLD

"The first part of the preparation should be employed in casting off the spirit of the world, which is contrary to that of Jesus Christ."

The spirit of the world consists essentially in the denial of the supreme dominion of God, a denial which is manifested in practice by sin and disobedience; thus, it is principally opposed to the spirit of Christ, which is also that of Mary.

It manifests itself by the concupiscence of the flesh, by the concupiscence of the eyes, and by the pride of life; by disobedience to God's laws and the abuse of created things. Its works are, first, sin in all its forms; and then all else by which the devil leads to sin; works which bring error and darkness to the mind and seduction and corruption to the will. Its pomps are the splendor and the charms employed by the devil to render sin alluring in persons, places and things.

Prayers to be said every day: Veni, Creator. Ave Maris
  Stella.
Reading suitable for the twelve days: Gospel accord-
  ing to St. Matthew, Chapters 5, 6, 7.
  Imitation of Christ, Book I, Chapters 13, 18,
  25; Book III, Chapters 10, 40.
Spiritual Exercises: Examine your conscience, pray,
  practice renouncement, mortification, purity
  of heart; this purity is the indispensable
  condition for contemplating God in
  Heaven, to see Him on earth and to know
  Him by the light of faith.

—SECOND PERIOD—

First Week
KNOWLEDGE OF SELF

"During the first week, they should employ all
their prayers and pious actions in asking for a
knowledge of themselves and for contrition for
their sins; and they should do this in a spirit of
humility."

During this week, we shall consider not so
much the opposition that exists between the spirit
of Jesus and ours, as the miserable and humiliat-

ing state to which our sins have reduced us. Moreover, the True Devotion being an easy, short, sure and perfect way to arrive at that union with Our Lord which is Christian perfection, we shall enter seriously upon this way, strongly convinced of our misery and helplessness. But how attain this without a knowledge of ourselves?

Prayers: Litany of the Holy Ghost. *Ave Maris Stella.* Litany of the Blessed Virgin Mary.

Reading: Gospel according to St. Matthew, Chapters 24, 25.

Gospel of St. Luke, Chapters 11,13,16,17,18.

Imitation of Christ, Book I, Chapter 24; Book II, Chapter 5; Book III, Chapters 7, 8, 13, 20, 30, 47.

Treatise on True Devotion (True Devotion to Mary), Nos. 78-82, 227, 228.

Spiritual Exercises: Prayers, examens, reflection, acts of renouncement of our own will, of contrition for our sins, of contempt of self —all performed at the feet of Mary, for it is from her we hope for light to know ourselves, and it is near her that we shall be able to measure the abyss of our miseries without despairing.

Second Week
KNOWLEDGE OF THE BLESSED VIRGIN

"They shall devote the second week to the knowledge of the Blessed Virgin."

We must unite ourselves to Jesus through Mary—this is the characteristic of our devotion; therefore, St. Louis De Montfort asks that the second week be employed in acquiring a knowledge of the Blessed Virgin.

Mary is our sovereign and our mediatrix, our Mother and our mistress. Let us then endeavor to know the effects of this royalty, of this mediation, and of this maternity, as well as the grandeurs and prerogatives which are the foundation or consequences thereof. Our Mother is also a perfect mold wherein we are to be molded in order to make her intentions and dispositions ours. This we cannot achieve without studying the interior life of Mary; namely, her virtues, her sentiments, her actions, her participation in the mysteries of Christ and her union with Him.

Prayers: Litany of the Holy Ghost. *Ave Maris Stella.* Litany of the Blessed Virgin Mary. St. Louis De Montfort's Prayer to Mary. Recitation of the Rosary.

Reading: Gospel according to St. Luke, Chap. 1, 2.

Gospel according to St. John, Chapter 2.

Treatise on True Devotion, Nos. 1-48, 90-93, 105-182, 213-225.

Secret of Mary, Nos. 23-34.

Spiritual Exercises: Acts of love, pious affections for the Blessed Virgin, imitation of her virtues, especially her profound humility, her lively faith, her blind obedience, her continual mental prayer, her mortification in all things, her divine purity, her ardent charity, her heroic patience, her angelic sweetness and her divine wisdom—"these being," as St. Louis De Montfort says, "the ten principal virtues of the Blessed Virgin."

Third Week
KNOWLEDGE OF JESUS CHRIST

"During the third week, they shall apply themselves to the study of Jesus Christ."

What is to be studied in Christ? First the man-God, His grace and glory; then His rights to sovereign dominion over us, since, after having renounced Satan and the world, we have taken Jesus Christ for our "Lord." What next shall be the object of our study? His exterior actions and also His interior life; namely, the virtues and acts of His Sacred Heart; His association with Mary in the mysteries of the Annunciation and Incarnation, during His infancy and hidden life, at the feast of Cana and on Calvary.

Prayers: Litany of the Holy Ghost. *Ave Maris Stella.* Litany of the Holy Name of Jesus or of the Sacred Heart. St. Louis De Montfort's Prayer to Jesus. *O Jesus living in Mary.*

Reading: Gospel according to St. Matthew, Chapters 26, 27.

Gospel according to St. John, Chapters 13 ff.

Imitation of Christ, Book II, Chapters 7,11,12; Book III, Chapters 5, 6, 56; Book IV, Chapters 1, 8, 13.

Treatise on True Devotion, Nos. 60-67, 183, 212, 226-265.

Spiritual Exercises: Acts of love of God, thanksgiving for the blessings of Jesus, contrition and resolution.

—PRAYERS—

Veni, Creator

Come, O Creator Spirit blest!
And in our souls take up Thy rest;
Come with Thy grace and heavenly aid,
To fill the hearts which Thou hast made.

Great Paraclete! To Thee we cry,
O highest gift of God most high!
O font of life! O fire of love!
And sweet anointing from above.

Thou in Thy sevenfold gifts art known,
The finger of God's hand we own;
The promise of the Father, Thou!
Who dost the tongue with power endow.

Kindle our senses from above,
And make our hearts o'erflow with love;
With patience firm and virtue high,
The weakness of our flesh supply.

Far from us drive the foe we dread,
And grant us Thy true peace instead;
So shall we not, with Thee for guide,
Turn from the path of life aside.

Oh, may Thy grace on us bestow
The Father and the Son to know,
And Thee through endless times confessed
Of both the Eternal Spirit blest.

All glory while the ages run
Be to the Father and the Son
Who rose from death; the same to Thee,
O Holy Ghost, eternally. Amen.

Magnificat

My soul doth magnify the Lord.

And my spirit hath rejoiced in God my Saviour.

Because He hath regarded the humility of His handmaid; for behold, from henceforth all generations shall call me blessed.

Because He that is mighty hath done great things to me, and holy is His name.

And His mercy is from generation unto generations, to them that fear Him.

He hath showed might in His arm; He hath scattered the proud in the conceit of their heart.

He hath put down the mighty from their seat and hath exalted the humble.

He hath filled the hungry with good things, and the rich He hath sent empty away.

He hath received Israel His servant, being mindful of His mercy:

As He spoke to our fathers, to Abraham and to his seed forever. Amen.

Glory be to the Father, and to the Son, and to the Holy Ghost, as it was in the beginning, is now, and ever shall be, world without end. Amen.

Ave Maris Stella

Hail, bright star of ocean,
God's own Mother blest,

Ever sinless Virgin,
Gate of heavenly rest.

Taking that sweet Ave,
Which from Gabriel came,
Peace confirm within us,
Changing Eva's name.

Break the captives' fetters,
Light on blindness pour,
All our ills expelling
Every bliss implore.

Show thyself a Mother;
May the Word Divine,
Born for us thine Infant,
Hear our prayers through thine.

Virgin all excelling,
Mildest of the mild,
Freed from guilt, preserve us
Pure and undefiled.

Keep our life all spotless,
Make our way secure,
Till we find in Jesus
Joy forevermore.

Through the highest Heaven
To the Almighty Three,
Father, Son and Spirit,
One same glory be. Amen.

Litany of the Holy Ghost
(For private use only)

Lord, have mercy on us.
  Christ, have mercy on us.
Lord, have mercy on us. Father all powerful,
  Have mercy on us.
Jesus, Eternal Son of the Father, Redeemer of the
  world, *save us.*
Spirit of the Father and the Son, boundless Life of
  both, *sanctify us.*
Holy Trinity, *hear us.*

Holy Ghost, Who proceeds from the Father and
  the Son, *enter our hearts.*
Holy Ghost, Who art equal to the Father and the
  Son, *enter our hearts.*
Promise of God the Father, *have mercy on us.*
Ray of heavenly light, *have mercy on us.*
Author of all good, *etc.*
Source of heavenly water,
Consuming Fire,
Ardent Charity,
Spiritual Unction,
Spirit of love and truth,
Spirit of wisdom and understanding,
Spirit of counsel and fortitude,
Spirit of knowledge and piety,

Spirit of the fear of the Lord,
Spirit of grace and prayer,
Spirit of peace and meekness,
Spirit of modesty and innocence,
Holy Ghost, the Comforter,
Holy Ghost, the Sanctifier,
Holy Ghost, Who governs the Church,
Gift of God the Most High,
Spirit Who fills the universe,
Spirit of the adoption of the children of God,

Holy Ghost, *inspire us with horror of sin.*
Holy Ghost, *come and renew the face of the earth.*
Holy Ghost, *shed Thy light into our souls.*
Holy Ghost, *engrave Thy law in our hearts.*
Holy Ghost, *inflame us with the flame of Thy love.*
Holy Ghost, *open to us the treasures of Thy graces.*
Holy Ghost, *teach us to pray well.*
Holy Ghost, *enlighten us with Thy heavenly inspirations.*
Holy Ghost, *lead us in the way of salvation.*
Holy Ghost, *grant us the only necessary knowledge.*
Holy Ghost, *inspire in us the practice of good.*
Holy Ghost, *grant us the merits of all virtues.*
Holy Ghost, *make us persevere in justice.*
Holy Ghost, *be Thou our everlasting reward.*

Lamb of God, Who takes away the sins of the world, *send us Thy Holy Ghost.*

Lamb of God, Who takes away the sins of the world, *pour down into our souls the gifts of the Holy Ghost.*

Lamb of God, Who takes away the sins of the world, *grant us the Spirit of wisdom and piety.*

V. Come, Holy Ghost! Fill the hearts of Thy faithful,

R. *And enkindle in them the fire of Thy love.*

Let Us Pray

Grant, O merciful Father, that Thy Divine Spirit may enlighten, inflame and purify us, that He may penetrate us with His heavenly dew and make us fruitful in good works, through Our Lord Jesus Christ, Thy Son, who with Thee, in the unity of the same Spirit, lives and reigns forever and ever. R. *Amen.*

Litany of the Blessed Virgin Mary
(For public or private use)

Lord, have mercy on us.
  Christ, have mercy on us.
Lord, have mercy on us. Christ, hear us.
  Christ, graciously hear us.
God the Father of Heaven,
  Have mercy on us.
God the Son, Redeemer of the world,
  Have mercy on us.
God the Holy Ghost,
  Have mercy on us.
Holy Trinity, One God,
  Have mercy on us.

Holy Mary, *pray for us.*
Holy Mother of God, *pray for us.*
Holy Virgin of virgins, *etc.*
Mother of Christ,
Mother of divine grace,
Mother most pure,
Mother most chaste,
Mother inviolate,
Mother undefiled,
Mother most amiable,
Mother most admirable,
Mother of good counsel,
Mother of our Creator,

Mother of our Saviour,
Virgin most prudent,
Virgin most venerable,
Virgin most renowned,
Virgin most powerful,
Virgin most merciful,
Virgin most faithful,
Mirror of justice,
Seat of wisdom,
Cause of our joy,
Spiritual vessel,
Vessel of honor,
Singular vessel of devotion,
Mystical rose,
Tower of David,
Tower of ivory,
House of gold,
Ark of the Covenant,
Gate of Heaven,
Morning star,
Health of the sick,
Refuge of sinners,
Comforter of the afflicted,
Help of Christians,
Queen of angels,
Queen of patriarchs,
Queen of prophets,
Queen of apostles,

Queen of martyrs,

Queen of confessors,

Queen of virgins,

Queen of all saints,

Queen conceived without original sin,

Queen assumed into Heaven,

Queen of the most holy Rosary,

Queen of peace,

Lamb of God, Who takes away the sins of the world, *spare us, O Lord.*

Lamb of God, Who takes away the sins of the world, *graciously hear us, O Lord.*

Lamb of God, Who takes away the sins of the world, *have mercy on us.*

V. Pray for us, O holy Mother of God,

R. *That we may be made worthy of the promises of Christ.*

Let Us Pray

Grant, we beseech Thee, O Lord God, that we Thy servants may enjoy perpetual health of mind and body, and by the glorious intercession of the Blessed Mary, ever Virgin, be delivered from present sorrow and enjoy everlasting happiness. Through Christ Our Lord. R. *Amen.*

St. Louis De Montfort's Prayer to Mary

Hail Mary, beloved Daughter of the Eternal Father! Hail Mary, admirable Mother of the Son! Hail Mary, faithful Spouse of the Holy Ghost! Hail Mary, my dear Mother, my loving mistress, my powerful sovereign! Hail my joy, my glory, my heart and my soul! Thou art all mine by mercy, and I am all thine by justice. But I am not yet sufficiently thine. I now give myself wholly to thee without keeping anything back for myself or others. If thou still seest in me anything which does not belong to thee, I beseech thee to take it, and to make thyself the absolute mistress of all that is mine. Destroy in me all that may be displeasing to God, root it up and bring it to nought; place and cultivate in me everything that is pleasing to thee.

May the light of thy faith dispel the darkness of my mind; may thy profound humility take the place of my pride; may thy sublime contemplation check the distractions of my wandering imagination; may thy continuous sight of God fill my memory with His presence; may the burning love of thy heart inflame the lukewarmness of mine; may thy virtues take the place of my sins; may thy merits be my only adornment in the sight of God and make up for all that is wanting in me. Finally, dearly beloved Mother, grant, if it be possible, that I may have no other spirit but thine, to know Jesus and His divine will; that I may have no other soul but thine, to praise and glorify the Lord; that I may have no other heart but thine, to love God with a love as pure and ardent as thine. I do not ask thee for visions, revelations, sensible devotion or spiritual pleasures. It is thy privilege to see God clearly; it is thy privilege to enjoy heavenly bliss; it is thy privilege to triumph gloriously in Heaven at the right hand of thy Son and to hold absolute sway over angels, men and demons; it is thy privilege to dispose of all the gifts of God, just as thou willest.

Such is, O heavenly Mary, the "best part," which the Lord has given thee and which shall never be taken away from thee, and this thought fills my heart with joy. As for my part here below, I wish for no other than that which was thine: to believe sincerely without spiritual pleasures; to suffer joyfully without human consolation; to die continually to myself without respite; and to work zealously and unselfishly for thee until death as the humblest of thy servants. The only grace I beg thee to obtain for me is that every day and every moment of my life I may say: "Amen, so be it, to all that thou didst do while on earth. Amen, so be it, to all that thou art now doing in Heaven.

Amen, so be it, to all that thou art doing in my soul, so that thou alone mayest fully glorify Jesus in me for time and eternity." Amen.

Litany of the Holy Name of Jesus
(For public or private use)

Lord, have mercy on us.
Christ, have mercy on us.
Lord, have mercy on us. Jesus, hear us.
Jesus, graciously hear us.
God the Father of Heaven,
Have mercy on us.
God the Son, Redeemer of the world,
Have mercy on us.
God the Holy Ghost,
Have mercy on us.
Holy Trinity, One God,
Have mercy on us.

Jesus, Son of the living God,
Have mercy on us.
Jesus, splendor of the Father,
Have mercy on us.
Jesus, brightness of eternal light, *etc.*
Jesus, King of glory,
Jesus, Sun of justice,

Jesus, Son of the Virgin Mary,
Jesus, most amiable,
Jesus, most admirable,
Jesus, mighty God,
Jesus, Father of the world to come,
Jesus, Angel of great counsel,
Jesus, most powerful,
Jesus, most patient,
Jesus, most obedient,
Jesus, meek and humble of heart,
Jesus, Lover of chastity,
Jesus, Lover of us,
Jesus, God of peace,
Jesus, Author of life,
Jesus, Model of virtues,
Jesus, zealous for souls,
Jesus, our God,
Jesus, our Refuge,
Jesus, Father of the poor,
Jesus, Treasure of the faithful,
Jesus, Good Shepherd,
Jesus, true Light,
Jesus, eternal Wisdom,
Jesus, infinite Goodness,
Jesus, our Way and our Life,
Jesus, Joy of Angels,
Jesus, King of Patriarchs,
Jesus, Master of Apostles,

Jesus, Teacher of Evangelists,
Jesus, Strength of Martyrs,
Jesus, Light of Confessors,
Jesus, Purity of Virgins,
Jesus, Crown of all Saints,

Be merciful,
  Spare us, O Jesus.
Be merciful,
  Graciously hear us, O Jesus.

From all evil, *deliver us, O Jesus.*
From all sin, *deliver us, O Jesus.*
From Thy wrath, *etc.*
From the snares of the devil,
From the spirit of fornication,
From everlasting death,
From the neglect of Thine inspirations,
Through the mystery of Thy holy Incarnation,
Through Thy Nativity,
Through Thine Infancy,
Through Thy most divine life,
Through Thy labors,
Through Thine Agony and Passion,
Through Thy Cross and dereliction,
Through Thy faintness and weariness,
Through Thy death and burial,
Through Thy Resurrection,
Through Thine Ascension,

Through Thine institution of the Most Holy
  Eucharist,
Through Thy joys,
Through Thy glory,

Lamb of God, Who takest away the sins of the
  world, *spare us, O Jesus.*
Lamb of God, Who takest away the sins of the
  world, *graciously hear us, O Jesus.*
Lamb of God, Who takest away the sins of the
  world, *have mercy on us, O Jesus.*

V. Jesus, hear us.
R. *Jesus, graciously hear us.*

Let Us Pray

O Lord Jesus Christ, Who hast said: "Ask and
ye shall receive; seek, and ye shall find; knock, and
it shall be opened unto you"; grant, we beseech
Thee, to us who ask, the gift of Thy most divine
love, that we may ever love Thee with all our heart
and in all our words and actions, and never cease
from praising Thee.

Make us, O Lord, to have both a perpetual fear
and love of Thy holy name, for Thou never failest
to govern those whom Thou foundest upon the
strength of Thy love, Who livest and reignest,
world without end. R. *Amen.*

Litany of the Sacred Heart of Jesus
(For public or private use)

Lord, have mercy on us.
  Christ, have mercy on us.
Lord, have mercy on us. Christ, hear us.
  Christ, graciously hear us.
God the Father of Heaven,
  Have mercy on us.
God the Son, Redeemer of the world,
  Have mercy on us.
God the Holy Ghost,
  Have mercy on us.
Holy Trinity, One God,
  Have mercy on us.

Heart of Jesus, Son of the Eternal Father,
  Have mercy on us.
Heart of Jesus, formed by the Holy Ghost in the
  womb of the Virgin Mother,
  Have mercy on us.
Heart of Jesus, substantially united to the Word of
  God, *etc.*
Heart of Jesus, of infinite majesty,
Heart of Jesus, holy Temple of God,
Heart of Jesus, Tabernacle of the Most High,
Heart of Jesus, House of God and Gate of Heaven,
Heart of Jesus, burning Furnace of charity,
Heart of Jesus, Vessel of justice and love,

Heart of Jesus, full of goodness and love,

Heart of Jesus, Abyss of all virtues,

Heart of Jesus, most worthy of all praise,

Heart of Jesus, King and center of all hearts,

Heart of Jesus, in Whom are all the treasures of wisdom and knowledge,

Heart of Jesus, in Whom dwells all the fullness of the divinity,

Heart of Jesus, in Whom the Father was well pleased,

Heart of Jesus, of Whose fullness we have all received,

Heart of Jesus, desire of the everlasting hills,

Heart of Jesus, patient and abounding in mercy,

Heart of Jesus, rich unto all who call upon Thee,

Heart of Jesus, Fountain of life and holiness,

Heart of Jesus, Propitiation for our sins,

Heart of Jesus, filled with reproaches,

Heart of Jesus, bruised for our offenses,

Heart of Jesus, made obedient unto death,

Heart of Jesus, pierced with a lance,

Heart of Jesus, Source of all consolation,

Heart of Jesus, our Life and Resurrection,

Heart of Jesus, our Peace and Reconciliation,

Heart of Jesus, Victim for our sins,

Heart of Jesus, Salvation of those who hope in Thee,

Heart of Jesus, Hope of those who die in Thee,

Heart of Jesus, Delight of all the Saints,

Lamb of God, Who takest away the sins of the world, *spare us, O Lord.*
Lamb of God, Who takest away the sins of the world, *graciously hear us, O Lord.*
Lamb of God, Who takest away the sins of the world, *have mercy on us.*

V. Jesus meek and humble of heart,
R. *Make our hearts like unto Thine.*

Let Us Pray

Almighty and eternal God, consider the Heart of Thy well-beloved Son and the praises and satisfaction He offers Thee in the name of sinners; appeased by worthy homage, pardon those who implore Thy mercy, in the name of the same Jesus Christ Thy Son, Who lives and reigns with Thee, world without end. R. *Amen.*

St. Louis De Montfort's Prayer to Jesus

O most loving Jesus, deign to let me pour forth my gratitude before Thee for the grace Thou hast bestowed upon me in giving me to Thy holy Mother through the devotion of holy slavery, that she may be my advocate in the presence of Thy Majesty and my support in my extreme misery. Alas, O Lord! I am so wretched that, without this dear Mother, I should be certainly lost. Yes, Mary is necessary for me at Thy side and everywhere: that she may appease Thy just wrath, because I have so often offended Thee; that she may save me from the eternal punishment of Thy justice, which I deserve; that she may contemplate Thee, speak to Thee, pray to Thee, approach Thee and please Thee; that she may help me to save my soul and the souls of others; in short, Mary is necessary for me that I may always do Thy holy will and seek Thy greater glory in all things. Ah, would that I could proclaim throughout the whole world the mercy that Thou hast shown to me! Would that everyone might know I should be already damned, were it not for Mary! Would that I might offer worthy thanksgiving for so great a blessing! Mary is in me. Oh, what a treasure! Oh, what a consolation! And shall I not be entirely hers? Oh, what ingratitude! My dear

Saviour, send me death rather than such a calamity, for I would rather die than live without belonging entirely to Mary. With St. John the Evangelist at the foot of the Cross, I have taken her a thousand times for my own and as many times have given myself to her; but if I have not yet done it as Thou, dear Jesus, dost wish, I now renew this offering as Thou dost desire me to renew it. And if Thou seest in my soul or my body anything that does not belong to this august princess, I pray Thee to take it and cast it far from me, for whatever in me does not belong to Mary is unworthy of Thee.

O Holy Spirit, grant me all these graces. Plant in my soul the Tree of true Life, which is Mary; cultivate it and tend it so that it may grow and blossom and bring forth the fruit of life in abundance. O Holy Spirit, give me great devotion to Mary, Thy faithful spouse; give me great confidence in her maternal heart and an abiding refuge in her mercy, so that by her Thou mayest truly form in me Jesus Christ, great and mighty, unto the fullness of His perfect age. Amen.

O Jesus, Living in Mary

O Jesus, living in Mary,
Come and live in Thy servants,
In the spirit of Thy holiness,
In the fullness of Thy might,
In the truth of Thy virtues,
In the perfection of Thy ways,
In the communion of Thy mysteries.
Subdue every hostile power
In Thy spirit, for the glory of the Father. Amen.

REGARDING THE CONSECRATION

"At the end of the three weeks," says St. Louis De Montfort, "they shall go to Confession and to Communion, with the intention of giving themselves to Jesus Christ in the quality of slaves of love by the hands of Mary. After Communion, which they should try to make according to the method given further on, they should recite the formula of their consecration, which they will also find further on. They ought to write it, or have it written, unless they have a printed copy of it; and they should sign it the same day they have made it.

"It would be well also that on that day they should pay some tribute to Jesus Christ and our Blessed Lady, either as a penance for their past unfaithfulness to the vows of their Baptism or as a testimony of their dependence on the dominion of Jesus and Mary. This tribute ought to be according to the devotion and ability of everyone, such as a fast, a mortification, an alms or a candle. If they had but a pin to give in homage, yet gave it with good heart, it would be enough for Jesus, who looks only at one's good will.[1]

"Once a year at least, on the same day, they should renew the same consecration, observing the same practices during the three weeks. They might also once a month, or even once a day, renew all they have done in these few words:

"'I am all Thine, and all that I have belongs to Thee, O my sweet Jesus, through Mary, Thy holy Mother.'"

Act of Consecration to Jesus Christ, the Incarnate Wisdom, through the Blessed Virgin Mary

O ETERNAL and Incarnate Wisdom! O sweetest and most adorable Jesus! True God and true man, only Son of the Eternal Father and of Mary ever virgin! I adore Thee profoundly

---

1. It is recommended that persons making the consecration register as members of the Confraternity of Mary, Queen of All Hearts.

in the bosom and splendors of Thy Father during eternity, and I adore Thee also in the virginal bosom of Mary, Thy most worthy Mother, in the time of Thine Incarnation.

I give Thee thanks for that Thou hast annihilated Thyself, taking the form of a slave, in order to rescue me from the cruel slavery of the devil. I praise and glorify Thee because Thou hast been pleased to submit Thyself to Mary, Thy holy Mother, in all things, in order to make me Thy faithful slave through her. But, alas! Ungrateful and faithless as I have been, I have not kept the promises which I made so solemnly to Thee in my Baptism; I have not fulfilled my obligations; I do not deserve to be called Thy child, nor yet Thy slave; and as there is nothing in me which does not merit Thine anger and Thy repulse, I dare not come by myself before Thy most holy and august Majesty. It is on this account that I have recourse to the intercession of Thy most holy Mother, whom Thou hast given me for a mediatrix with Thee. It is through her that I hope to obtain of Thee contrition, the pardon of my sins, and the acquisition and preservation of wisdom.

Hail, then, O Immaculate Mary, living tabernacle of the Divinity, where the Eternal Wisdom willed to be hidden and to be adored by Angels and by men! Hail, O Queen of Heaven and earth, to whose empire everything is subject which is under God. Hail, O sure refuge of sinners, whose mercy fails no one. Hear the desires which I have of the Divine Wisdom; and for that end receive the vows and offerings which in my lowliness I present to thee.

I, (*name*), a faithless sinner, renew and ratify today in thy hands the vows of my Baptism; I renounce forever Satan, his pomps and works; and I give myself entirely to Jesus Christ, the Incarnate Wisdom, to carry my cross after Him all the days of my life and to be more faithful to Him than I have ever been before.

In the presence of all the Heavenly Court, I choose thee this day for my Mother and mistress. I deliver and consecrate to thee, as thy slave, my body and soul, my goods, both interior and exterior, and even the value of all my good actions—past, present and future—leaving to thee the entire and full right of disposing of me and all that belongs to me, without exception, according to thy good pleasure, for the greater glory of God, in time and in eternity.

Receive, O benignant Virgin, this little offering of my slavery, in honor of and in union with that subjection which the Eternal Wisdom deigned to have to thy maternity, in homage to the power which both of you have over this poor sinner and in thanksgiving for the privileges with which the Holy Trinity has favored thee. I declare that I wish henceforth, as thy true slave, to seek thy honor and to obey thee in all things.

O admirable Mother, present me to thy dear Son as His eternal slave, so that as He has redeemed me by thee, by thee He may receive me! O Mother of Mercy, grant me the grace to obtain the true Wisdom of God, and for that end receive me among those whom thou dost love and teach, whom thou dost lead, nourish and protect as thy children and thy slaves.

O faithful Virgin, make me in all things so perfect a disciple, imitator and slave of the Incarnate Wisdom, Jesus Christ thy Son, that I may attain, by thine intercession and by thine example, to the fullness of His age on earth and of His glory in Heaven. Amen.

—Part III—

THE CONFRATERNITY
OF MARY,
QUEEN OF ALL HEARTS

THE CONFRATERNITY OF MARY, QUEEN OF ALL HEARTS

It is not necessary to join any religious group in order to make and live St. Louis De Montfort's Consecration to Jesus through Mary. However, those who so desire may join the Confraternity of Mary, Queen of All Hearts (a religious group which the Church classifies as a "pious union" of the faithful).

The Confraternity of Mary, Queen of All Hearts, was first established on March 25, 1899. Pope St. Pius X erected it as an Archconfraternity in Rome on April 28, 1913.

Today there are eighty-eight branches of the Confraternity in various parts of the world: the United States, Canada, Haiti, South America, Europe, Asia and Africa. There are several hundred thousand members throughout the world.

OBJECT

The object of the Confraternity of Mary, Queen of All Hearts, is to establish within us the reign of Mary as a means of establishing more perfectly the reign of Jesus in our souls.

CONDITIONS OF MEMBERSHIP

(1) Prepare yourself and make the Act of Consecration to Jesus through Mary on a special day, preferably a feast of Our Lady.

(2) Send in your name to be recorded in the official register by the Director, who will send you a membership leaflet.

(3) It is commendable to make a small offering or to do a good work in honor of Our Lady on the day of Consecration. "It would be well," says St. Louis De Montfort, "that on that day they should pay some tribute to Jesus Christ and our Blessed Lady. . . . This tribute ought to be according to the devotion and ability of each one, such as a fast, a mortification, an alms or a candle."

(4) Wear the medal of Our Lady, Queen of All Hearts. This is not required of those who wear a crucifix in some ostensible manner.

Important: Only those may become members who understand and practice the "Perfect Devotion" to the Blessed Virgin explained by St. Louis De Montfort in the book *True Devotion to the Blessed Virgin* and in the booklet *The Secret of Mary.*

PRACTICES

Every morning, the members renew their Consecration to Jesus through Mary, at least by using the short formula: "I am all Thine, and all I have is Thine, O most loving Jesus, through Mary, Thy holy Mother."

After that, they apply themselves zealously to live always in dependence on Mary and to do all their actions in union with her. This is the only obligation, and it will be easily fulfilled if, during the day, they renew from time to time the donation of themselves by repeating the short formula given above, or even by a mere interior act of the mind.

Other prayers most conformable to the spirit of the Confraternity, and therefore most highly recommended, are the *Rosary*, the *Angelus*, the *Litany of the Blessed Virgin*, the *Magnificat* and the *Little Crown of Our Lady*.

INDULGENCES

(1) Members may gain a plenary indulgence on the day of admission and the Feast of the Annunciation (Leo XIII, May 30, 1899); on the Feast of the Immaculate Conception and St. Louis De Montfort's Day, provided that the Act of Consecration be renewed (Pius X, December 24, 1907);

on Christmas Day, the Feast of the Purification, both feasts of Our Lady of Sorrows (the Friday after Passion Sunday and September 15), the Feast of the Visitation, the Feast of the Assumption and at the hour of death (Pius X, December 18, 1913).

The following conditions are required for the indulgence at the hour of death: that the sick person make acts of contrition and charity, that he be resigned to the Will of God and offer up his sufferings and death in atonement for his sins, and that he invoke the holy Name of Jesus, at least interiorly.

All the other plenary indulgences are applicable to the Souls in Purgatory and may be gained on the usual conditions of Confession, Communion and one *Our Father, Hail Mary* and *Glory Be* for the intentions of the Holy Father.

(2) A partial indulgence may be gained every time a member renews his Consecration with the prayer: "I am all Thine, and all I have is Thine, O most loving Jesus, through Mary, Thy holy Mother."

(3) A partial indulgence may be gained every time a member performs a good work in union with the Blessed Virgin.

Members of the Confraternity also share in the

satisfactions, prayers and good works of the Fathers of the Company of Mary (the Montfort Fathers) and the Daughters of Wisdom, the two congregations founded by St. Louis De Montfort.

FEASTS OF THE CONFRATERNITY

The Annunciation, March 25, is the principal feast of the Confraternity, because that is the day on which Our Lord came to us through Mary and set us an example of complete dependence on her. The secondary feast is that of St. Louis De Montfort, April 28.

Other special feasts are the Immaculate Conception, Christmas, the Visitation, the Purification, the Assumption and the Feast of St. John the Evangelist.

Correspondence regarding the Confraternity should be sent to

Rev. Father Director
The Confraternity
Montfort Fathers
26 South Saxon Ave.
Bay Shore, NY 11706

If you have enjoyed this book, consider making your next selection from among the following . . .

Religious Customs in the Family. *Fr. Weiser, S.J.* 8.00
St. Monica—Model of Christian Mothers. *Forbes*. . . . 6.00
Call to Souls. *Menendez* 1.00
St. Maximilian Kolbe. *Fr. Smith, O.F.M. Conv.* 6.00
St. Maria Goretti. *Fr. Poage, C.P.* 6.00
Secret of Mary. *St. Louis De Montfort.* 5.00
Mama! Why Did You Kill Us? *Mondrone* 2.00
Novena of Holy Communions. *Lovasik.* 2.00
The Forgotten Secret of Fatima 1.50
The Facts about Luther. *O'Hare* 16.50
Pope St. Pius X. *F. A. Forbes* 8.00
St. Alphonsus Liguori. *Miller & Aubin* 16.50
St. Teresa of Avila. *Walsh* 21.50
Therese Neumann—Mystic and Stigmatist. *Vogl.* 13.00
Life of the Blessed Virgin Mary. *Emmerich.* 16.50
The Way of Divine Love. (pocket, unabr.) *Sr. Menendez.* 8.50
Light and Peace. *Quadrupani.* 7.00
Where We Got the Bible. *Graham.* 6.00
Trustful Surrender to Divine Providence 5.00
Charity for the Suffering Souls. *Nageleisen* 16.50
The Voice of the Saints. (Sayings of) 6.00
Catholic Apologetics. *Laux* 10.00
The Devil—Does He Exist? *Delaporte* 6.00
A Catechism of Modernism. *Lemius* 5.00
St. Bernadette Soubirous. *Trochu* 18.50
The Love of Mary. *Roberto.* 8.00
A Prayerbook of Favorite Litanies. *Hebert* 10.00
The 12 Steps to Holiness and Salvation. *Liguori.* . . . 7.50
The Rosary and the Crisis of Faith. 2.00
Eucharistic Miracles. *Cruz* 15.00
The Blessed Virgin Mary. *St. Alphonsus* 4.50
Priest, the Man of God. *Cafasso* 12.50
Soul of the Apostolate. *Chautard* 10.00
Little Catechism of the Curé of Ars. *St. J. Vianney.* . . . 6.00
The Four Last Things. *von Cochem.* 7.00
The Cure of Ars. *O'Brien* 5.50
The Angels. *Parente* 9.00

Prices subject to change.

True Devotion to Mary. *St. Louis De Montfort* 8.00
Story of a Soul. *St. Therese*. 8.00
My Sister St. Therese. *Sr. Genevieve*. 8.00
Sermons of the Curé of Ars. *Vianney*. 12.50
Revelations of St. Bridget of Sweden. *St. Bridget* 3.00
St. Catherine Labouré of the Miraculous Medal. 13.50
St. Therese, The Little Flower. *Beevers*. 6.00
Purgatory Explained. (pocket, unabr.) *Fr. Schouppe* . . 9.00
Prophecy for Today. *Edward Connor* 5.50
What Will Hell Be Like? *St. Alphonsus Liguori* 75
Saint Michael and the Angels. *Approved Sources* 7.00
Modern Saints—Their Lives & Faces. Book I. *Ball* . . 18.00
Our Lady of Fatima's Peace Plan from Heaven 75
Divine Favors Granted to St. Joseph. *Pere Binet* 5.00
Catechism of the Council of Trent. *McHugh/Callan* . . 24.00
Padre Pio—The Stigmatist. *Fr. Charles Carty*. 15.00
Fatima—The Great Sign. *Francis Johnston*. 8.00
The Incorruptibles. *Joan Carroll Cruz* 13.50
St. Anthony—The Wonder Worker of Padua 5.00
The Holy Shroud & Four Visions. *Fr. O'Connell*. 2.00
The Secret of the Rosary. *St. Louis De Montfort* 3.00
Confession of a Roman Catholic. *Paul Whitcomb* 1.50
The Catholic Church Has the Answer. *Whitcomb* 1.50
I Wait for You. *Sr. Josefa Menendez* 75
Words of Love. *Menendez, Betrone, etc.*. 6.00
Little Lives of the Great Saints. *Murray* 18.00
Prayer—The Key to Salvation. *Fr. M. Müller.* 7.50
Sermons on Our Lady. *St. Francis de Sales*. 10.00
Sermons of St. Alphonsus Liguori for Every Sun. 16.50
Alexandrina—The Agony and the Glory 6.00
Life of Blessed Margaret of Castello. *Fr. W. Bonniwell* 7.50
St. Francis of Paola. *Simi and Segreti*. 8.00
Bible History of the Old and New Tests. *Schuster*. . . . 10.00
Dialogue of St. Catherine of Siena. 10.00
Dolorous Passion of Our Lord. *Emmerich*. 16.50
Textual Concordance of the Holy Scriptures 35.00
Douay-Rheims Bible. *Leatherbound.* 35.00

—At your Bookdealer or direct from the Publisher.—
Call Toll-Free 1-800-437-5876.

Prices subject to change.

ORDER FORM

TAN BOOKS AND PUBLISHERS, INC.
P.O. Box 424
Rockford, Illinois 61105
TOLL FREE 1-800-437-5876

Gentlemen:

Please send me _____ copies of THE SECRET OF MARY by St. Louis De Montfort.

☐ Enclosed is my payment in the amount of

_____.

☐ Please charge to:

    ☐ VISA   ☐ MasterCard   ☐ Discover

My account number: _____

Expiration date: Month _____ Year _____

Account Name _____

Signature _____
                  (Do not send us your card.)

Name _____

Street _____

City _____

State _____ Zip _____

Please include postage and handling according to the following: For orders of $1-$10, add $2; $10.01-$20, add $3; $20.01-$30, add $4.00; $30.01-$50, add $5.00; $50.01-$75, add $6.00; $75.01-up, add $7.00. Illinois residents add 6% Sales Tax. All foreign customers please remit in U.S. funds. Overseas customers add 20% of your order for surface postage.

Consecration to the Blessed Virgin Mary is crucial to effecting a change in our sinful and misguided world today. Mary alone has a promise from God of victory over Satan (*Gen.* 3:15), and at Fatima she promised the triumph of her Immaculate Heart and a period of peace for the world. Therefore this little book can be a major key to hastening the reign of her Heart and to the saving of countless souls. We are making it available at the lowest possible prices, that apostolic-minded people might better be able to place it in as many hands as possible. The issue is the salvation of souls and peace in the world.

Quantity Discount

1 copy	5.00		
5 copies	3.00	each	15.00 total
10 copies	2.50	each	25.00 total
25 copies	2.25	each	56.25 total
50 copies	2.00	each	100.00 total
100 copies	1.75	each	175.00 total
500 copies	1.50	each	750.00 total
1,000 copies	1.40	each	1,400.00 total

See over for postage and handling.

Priced low purposely for wide distribution.